POETRY FROM CRESCENT MOON

William Shakespeare: *Selected Sonnets and Verse*
edited, with an introduction by Mark Tuley

William Shakespeare: *The Sonnets*
edited and introduced by Mark Tuley

*Shakespeare: Love, Poetry and Magic
in Shakespeare's Sonnets and Plays*
by B.D. Barnacle

Edmund Spenser: *Heavenly Love: Selected Poems*
selected and introduced by Teresa Page

Robert Herrick: *Delight In Disorder: Selected Poems*
edited and introduced by M.K. Pace

Sir Thomas Wyatt: *Love For Love: Selected Poems*
selected and introduced by Louise Cooper

John Donne: *Air and Angels: Selected Poems*
selected and introduced by A.H. Ninham

D.H. Lawrence: *Being Alive: Selected Poems*
edited with an introduction by Margaret Elvy

D.H. Lawrence: Symbolic Landscapes
by Jane Foster

D.H. Lawrence: Infinite Sensual Violence
by M.K. Pace

Percy Bysshe Shelley: *Paradise of Golden Lights: Selected Poems*
selected and introduced by Charlotte Greene

Thomas Hardy: *Her Haunting Ground: Selected Poems*
edited, with an introduction by A.H. Ninham

Sexing Hardy: Thomas Hardy and Feminism
by Margaret Elvy

Emily Bronte: *Darkness and Glory: Selected Poems*
selected and introduced by Miriam Chalk

John Keats: *Bright Star: Selected Poems*
edited with an introduction by Miriam Chalk

Henry Vaughan: *A Great Ring of Pure and Endless Light: Selected Poems*
selected and introduced by A.H. Ninham

The Crescent Moon Book of Love Poetry
edited by Louise Cooper

The Crescent Moon Book of Mystical Poetry in English
edited by Carol Appleby

The Crescent Moon Book of Nature Poetry From Langland to Lawrence
edited by Margaret Elvy

The Crescent Moon Book of Metaphysical Poetry
edited and introduced by Charlotte Greene

The Crescent Moon Book of Elizabethan Love Poetry
edited and introduced by Carol Appleby

The Crescent Moon Book of Romantic Poetry
edited and introduced by L.M. Poole

Blinded By Her Light The Love-Poetry of Robert Graves
by Jeremy Mark Robinson

The Best of Peter Redgrove's Poetry: The Book of Wonders
by Peter Redgrove, edited and introduced by Jeremy Mark Robinson

Peter Redgrove: Here Comes the Flood
by Jeremy Mark Robinson

Sex-Magic-Poetry-Cornwall: A Flood of Poems
by Peter Redgrove, edited with an essay by Jeremy Mark Robinson

Brigitte's Blue Heart
by Jeremy Reed

Claudia Schiffer's Red Shoes
by Jeremy Reed

By-Blows: Uncollected Poems
by D.J. Enright

Petrarch, Dante and the Troubadours: The Religion of Love and Poetry
by Cassidy Hughes

Dante: *Selections From the Vita Nuova*
translated by Thomas Okey

Arthur Rimbaud: *Selected Poems*
edited and translated by Andrew Jary

Arthur Rimbaud: *A Season in Hell*
edited and translated by Andrew Jary

Rimbaud: Arthur Rimbaud and the Magic of Poetry
by Jeremy Mark Robinson

Friedrich Hölderlin: *Hölderlin's Songs of Light: Selected Poems*
translated by Michael Hamburger

Rainer Maria Rilke: *Dance the Orange:* Selected Poems
translated by Michael Hamburger

Rilke: Space, Essence and Angels in the Poetry of Rainer Maria Rilke
by B.D. Barnacle

German Romantic Poetry: Goethe, Novalis, Heine, Hölderlin, Schlegel, Schiller
by Carol Appleby

Arseny Tarkovsky: *Life, Life: Selected Poems*
translated by Virginia Rounding

Emily Dickinson: *Wild Nights: Selected Poems*
selected and introduced by Miriam Chalk

Cavafy: Anatomy of a Soul
by Matt Crispin

Wild Nights
Selected Poems

Wild Nights
Selected Poems

Emily Dickinson

Edited by Miriam Chalk

CRESCENT MOON

CRESCENT MOON PUBLISHING
P.O. Box 393
Maidstone
Kent, ME14 5XU
United Kingdom

First published 1996. Second edition 2007
Introduction © Miriam Chalk, 1996, 2007.

Printed and bound in Great Britain.
Set in Garamond Book 12 on 18pt.
Designed by Radiance Graphics.

The right of Miriam Chalk to be identified as the editor of *Wild Nights: Selected Poems* has been asserted generally in accordance with sections 77 and 78 of the Copyright, Designs and Patents Act 1988.

All rights reserved. No part of this book may be reprinted or reproduced, stored in a retrieval system, or transmitted, in any form or by any means, electronic, mechanical, photocopying, recording or otherwise, without permission from the publisher.

British Library Cataloguing in Publication data available

ISBN 1-86171-146-8
ISBN-13 9781861711468

Contents

"A Light exists in Spring" 11
"The Sky is Low" 12
"The Lilac is an ancient shrub" 13
"Exhilaration is the Breeze" 14
"On this wondrous sea" 15
"To see the Summer Sky" 16
from "A Song to David" 17
"Behind me – dips Eternity" 18
"Wild Nights – Wild Nights!" 19
"A something in a summer's Day" 20
"'Tis so much joy! 'Tis so much joy!" 22
"Exultation is the going" 23
"Me – come! My dazzled face" 24
"Title divine – is mine!" 25
"Did Our Best Moment last" 26
"I gained it so" 27
"What would I give to see his face?" 28
"If you were coming in the Fall" 30
"To my small Hearth His fire came" 31
"It's all I have to bring today" 32
"I think I was enchanted" 33
"Unable are the Loved to die" 35
"When I hoped, I recollect" 36
"I cannot live with You" 38
"I hide myself within my flower" 41

"Were it to be the last" 42
"I never saw a Moor" 43
"Spring comes on the World" 44
"'Twas my one Glory" 45
"Victory comes late" 46
"To be alive - is Power" 47
"I dwell in Possibility" 48
"I've Known a Heaven" 49
"Tis wider than the Sky" 50
"It might be lonelier" 51
"Exhilaration - is within" 52
"It struck me - every Day" 53
"Lift - with the Feathers" 54
"Like Rain it sounded till it curved" 55
"A word is dead" 56
"Go travelling with us!" 57
"The Thrill came slowly like a Boon" 58
"And with what body do they come?" 59
"Lightly stepped a yellow star" 60
"Pass to thy Rendezvous of Light" 61
"To wait an Hour - is long" 62
"We outgrow love like other things" 63
"You left me, sweet, two legacies" 64
"This is my letter to the world" 65
"The pedigree of honey" 66
"Of all the souls that stand create" 67
"I like to see it lap the miles" 68
"To make a prairie" 69
"I taste a liquor never brewed" 70
"It's all I have to bring today" 71
"The Soul unto itself" 72
"It's like the light" 73

"There is a solitude of space" 74
"Beauty crowds me till I die" 75

A Note On Emily Dickinson 81

["A Light exists in Spring"]

A light exists in Spring
Not present on the Year
At any other period –
When March is scarcely here

A Color stands abroad
On Solitary Fields
That Science cannot overtake
But Human Nature feels.

It waits upon the Lawn,
It shows the furthest Tree
Upon the furthest Slope you know
It almost speaks to you.

Then as Horizons step
Or Noons report away
Without the Formula of sound
It passes and we stay –

A quality of loss
Affecting our Content
As Trade had suddenly encroached
Upon a Sacrament.

["The Sky is Low"]

The sky is low, the clouds are mean,
A travelling flake of snow
Across a barn or through a rut
Debates if it will go.

A narrow wind complains all day
How someone treated him;
Nature, like us, is sometimes caught
Without her diadem.

["The Lilac is an ancient shrub"]

The Lilac is an ancient shrub
But ancienter than that
The firmamental Lilac
Upon the Hill tonight -
The Sun subsiding on his Course
Bequeaths this final Plant
To Contemplation - not to Touch -
The Flower of Occident.
Of one Corolla is the West -
The Calyx is the Earth -
The Capsules burnished Seeds the Stars
The Scientist of Faith
His research has but just begun -
Above his synthesis
The Flora unimpeachable
To Time's Analysis -
"Eye hath not seen" may possibly
Be current with the Blind
But let not Revelation
By theses be detained -

["Exhilaration is the Breeze"]

Exhilaration is the Breeze
That lifts us from the Ground
And leaves us in another place
Whose statement is not found -

Returns us not, but after time
We soberly descend
A little newer for the term
Upon Enchanted Ground -

["On this wondrous sea"]

On this wondrous sea
Sailing silently,
Ho! Pilot, ho!
Knowest thou the shore
Where no breakers roar –
Where the storm is o'er?

In the peaceful west
Many the sails at rest –
The anchors fast –
Thither I pilot thee –
Land Ho! Eternity!
A shore at last!

["To see the Summer Sky"]

To see the Summer Sky
Is Poetry, though never in a Book it lie -
True Poems flee -

[*from* "A Song to David"]

Glorious the sun in mid career;
Glorious th' assembled fires appear;
    Glorious the comet's train:
Glorious the trumpet and alarm;
Glorious th' almighty stretch'd-out arm;
    Glorious th' enraptur'd main;

Glorious the northern lights astream;
Glorious the song, when God's the theme
    Glorious the thunder's roar:
Glorious hosanna from the den;
Glorious the catholic amen;
    Glorious the martyr's gore:

Glorious – more glorious is the crown
Of Him that brought salvation down
    By meekness, call'd thy Son;
Thou that stupendous truth believ'd,
And now the matchless deed's achiev'd,
    Determined, Dared, and Done.

["Behind me – dips Eternity"]

Behind me – dips Eternity –
Before Me – Immortality –
Myself – the Term between –
Death but the Drift of Eastern Gray,
Dissolving into Dawn away,
Before the West begin –

'Tis kingdoms – afterward – they say –
In perfect – pauseless Monarchy –
Whose Prince – is Son of None –
Himself – His Dateless Dynasty –
Himself – Himself diversify –
In Duplicate divine –

'Tis Miracle before Me – then –
'Tis Miracle behind – between –
A Crescent in the Sea –
With Midnight to the North of Her –
And Midnight to the South of Her –
And Maelstrom – in the Sky –

["Wild Nights - Wild Nights!"]

Wild Nights! - Wild Nights!
Were I with thee
Wild Nights should be
Our luxury!

Futile - the Winds -
To a Heart in port -
Done with the Compass -
Done with the Chart!

Rowing in Eden -
Ah, the sea!
Might I but moor - Tonight -
In Thee!

["A something in a summer's Day"]

A something in a summer's Day
As slow her flambeaux burn away
Which solemnizes me.

A something in a summer's noon -
A depth - an Azure - a perfume -
Transcending ecstasy.

And still within a summer's night
A something so transporting bright
I clap my hands to see -

Then veil my too inspecting face
Lest such a subtle - shimmering grace
Flutter too far for me -

The wizard fingers never rest -
The purple brook within the breast
Still chafes its narrow bed -

Still rears the East her amber Flag -
Guides still the Sun along the Crag
His Caravan of Red -

So looking on - the night - the morn
Conclude the wonder gay -
And I meet, coming thro' the dews
Another summer's Day!

["'Tis so much joy! 'Tis so much joy!"]

'Tis so much joy! 'Tis so much joy!
If I should fail, what poverty!
And yet, as poor as I,
Have ventured all upon a throw!
Have gained! Yes! Hesitated so -
This side the Victory!

Life is but Life! And Death, but Death!
Bliss is, but Bliss, and Breath but Breath!
And if indeed I fail,
At least to know the worst, is sweet!
Defeat means nothing but *Defeat,*
No drearier, can befall!

And if I gain! Oh Gun at Sea!
Oh Bells, that in the Steeples be!
At first, repeat it slow!
For Heaven is a different thing,
Conjectured, and waked sudden in -
And might extinguish me!

["Exultation is the going"]

*Exultation is the going
Of an inland soul to sea,
Past the houses - past the headlands -
Into deep Eternity -*

*Bred as we, among the mountains,
Can the sailor understand
The divine intoxication
Of the first league out from land?*

["Me - come! My dazzled face"]

Me - come! My dazzled face
In such a shining place!
Me - hear! My foreign Ear
The sounds of Welcome - there!

The Saints forget
Our bashful feet -

My Holiday, shall be
That They - remember me -
My Paradise - the fame
That They - pronounce my name -

["Title divine - is mine!"]

Title divine - is mine!
The Wife - without the sign!
Acute Degree - conferred on me -
Empress of Calvary!
Royal - all but the Crown!
Betrothed - without the swoon
God sends us Women -
When you - hold - Garnet to Garnet -
Gold - to Gold -
Born - Bridalled - Shrouded -
In a Day -
Tri Victory
"My Husband" - women say -
Stroking the Melody -
Is this - the way?

["Did Our Best Moment last"]

Did Our Best Moment last -
'Twould supersede the Heaven -
A few - and they by Risk - procure -
So this Sort - are not given -

Except as stimulants - in
Cases of Despair -
Or Stupor - The Reserve -
These heavenly Moments are -

A Grant of the Divine -
That Certain as it Comes -
Withdraws - and leaves the dazzled Soul
In her unfurnished Rooms

["I gained it so"]

I gained it so -
By Climbing slow -
By catching at the Twigs that grow
Between the Bliss - and me -
It hung so high
As well the Sky
Attempt by Strategy -

I said I gained it - This - was all -
Look, how I clutch it
Lest it fall -
And I a Pauper go
Unfitted by an instant's Grace
For the Contented - Beggar's face
I wore - an hour ago -

["What would I give to see his face?"]

What would I give to see his face?
I'd give - I'd give my life - of course -
But that *is not enough!*
Stop just a minute - let me think!
I'd give my biggest Bobolink!
That makes two *- Him -* and *Life!*
You know who "June" *is -*
I'd give her *-*
Roses a day from Zanzibar -
And Lily tubes - like Wells -
Bees - by the furlong -
Straits of Blue
Navies of Butterflies - sailed thro' -
And dappled Cowslip Dells -

Then I have "shares" in Primrose "Banks" -
Daffodil Dowries - spicy "Stocks" -
Dominions - broad as Dew -
Bags of Doubloons - adventurous Bees
Brought me - from firmamental seas -
And Purple - from Peru -

Now - *have I bought it -*
"Shylock"? - Say!
Sign me the Bond!
"I vow to pay
To Her - who pledges this -
One hour - *of her Sovereign's face"!*
Ecstatic *Contract!*
Niggard *Grace!*
My Kingdom's worth *of Bliss!*

["If you were coming in the Fall"]

If you were coming in the Fall,
I'd brush the Summer by
With half a smile, and half a spurn,
As Housewives do, a Fly.

If I could see you in a year,
I'd wind the months in balls -
And put them each in separate Drawers,
For fear the numbers fuse -

If only Centuries, delayed,
I'd count them on my Hand,
Subtracting, till my fingers dropped
Into Van Dieman's Land.

If certain, when this life was out -
That yours and mine, should be
I'd toss it yonder, like a Rain,
And take Eternity -

But now, uncertain of the length
Of this, that is between,
It goads me, like the Goblin Bee -
That will not state - its sting.

["To my small Hearth His fire came"]

To my small Hearth His fire came -
And all my House aglow
Did fan and rock, with sudden light -
'Twas Sunrise - 'twas the Sky -

Impanelled from no Summer brief -
With limit of Decay -
'Twas Noon - without the News of Night -
Nay, Nature, it was Day -

["It's all I have to bring today"]

It's all I have to bring today -
This, and my heart beside -
This, and my heart, and all the fields -
And all the meadows wide -
Be sure you count - should I forget
Someone the sum could tell -
This, and my heart, and all the Bees
Which in the Clover dwell.

["I think I was enchanted"]

*I think I was enchanted
When first a sombre Girl -
I read that Foreign Lady -
The Dark - felt beautiful -*

*And whether it was noon at night -
Or only Heaven - at Noon -
For very Lunacy of Light
I had not power to tell -*

*The Bees - became as Butterflies -
The Butterflies - as Swans -
Approached - and spurned the narrow Grass -
And just the meanest Tunes*

*That Nature murmured to herself
To keep herself in Cheer -
I took for Giants - practising
Titanic Opera -*

*The Days - to Mighty Metres stept -
The homeliest - adorned
As if unto a Jubilee*

'Twere suddenly confirmed -

I could not have defined the change -
Conversion of the Mind
Like Sanctifying in the Soul -
Is witnessed - not explained -

'Twas a Divine Insanity -
The Danger to be Sane
Should I again experience -
'Tis Antidote to turn -

To Tomes of solid witchcraft -
Magicians be asleep -
But Magic - hath an Element
Like Deity - to keep -

["Unable are the Loved to die"]

Unable are the Loved to die
For Love is Immortality,
Nay, it is Deity -

Unable they that love - to die
For Love reforms Vitality
Into Divinity.

["When I hoped, I recollect"]

When I hoped, I recollect
Just the place I stood -
At a Window facing West -
Roughest Air - was good -

Not a Sleet could bite me -
Not a frost could cool -
Hope it was that kept me warm -
Not Merino shawl -

When I feared - I recollect
Just the Day it was -
Worlds were lying out to Sun -
Yet how Nature froze -

Icicles upon my soul
Prickled Blue and Cool -
Bird went praising everywhere -
Only Me - was still -

And the Day that I despaired -
This - if I forget
Nature will - that it be Night

After Sun has set -
Darkness intersect her face -
And put out her eye -
Nature hesitate - before
Memory and I -

["I cannot live with You"]

I cannot live with You -
It would be Life -
And Life is over there -
Behind the Shelf

The Sexton keeps the Key to -
Putting up
Our Life - His Porcelain -
Like a Cup -

Discarded of the Housewife -
Quaint - or Broke -
A newer Sevres pleases -
Old Ones crack -

I could not die - with You -
For One must wait
To shut the Other's Gaze down -
You - could not -

And I - Could I stand by
And see You - freeze -
Without my Right of Frost -

Death's privilege?

Nor could I rise – with You –
Because Your Face
Would put out Jesus' –
That New Grace

Glow plain – and foreign
On my homesick Eye –
Except that You than He
Shone closer by –

They'd judge Us – How –
For You – served Heaven – You know,
Or sought to –
I could not –

Because You saturated Sight –
And I had no more Eyes
For sordid excellence
As Paradise

And were You lost, I would be –
Though My Name
Rang loudest
On the Heavenly fame –

And were You - saved -
And I - condemned to be
Where You were not -
That self - were Hell to Me -

So We must meet apart -
You there - I - here -
With just the Door ajar
That Oceans are - and Prayer -
And that White Sustenance -
Despair -

["I hide myself within my flower"]

I hide myself within my flower,
That fading from your Vase,
You, unsuspecting, feel for me –
Almost a loneliness.

["Were it to be the last"]

Were it to be the last
How infinite would be
What we did not suspect was marked –
Our final interview.

["I never saw a Moor"]

I never saw a Moor –
I never saw the Sea –
Yet know I how the Heather looks
And what a Billow be.

I never spoke with God
Nor visited in Heaven –
Yet certain am I of the spot
As if the Checks were given –

["Spring comes on the World"]

Spring comes on the World -
I sight the Aprils -
Hueless to me until thou come
As, till the Bee
Blossoms stand negative,
Touched to Conditions
By a Hum.

["'Twas my one Glory"]

'Twas my one Glory -
Let it be
Remembered
I was owned of Thee -

["Victory comes late"]

Victory comes late -
And is held low to freezing lips -
Too rapt with frost
To take it -
How sweet it would have tasted -
Just a Drop -
Was God so economical?
His Table's spread too high for Us -
Unless We dine on tiptoe -
Crumbs - fit such little mouths -
Cherries - suit Robins -
The eagle's Golden Breakfast strangles - Them -
God keep His Oath to Sparrows -
Who of little Love - know how to starve -

["To be alive - is Power"]

To be alive - is Power -
Existence - in itself -
Without a further function -
Omnipotence - Enough -
To be alive - and Will!
'Tis able as a God -
The Maker - of Ourselves - be what -
Such being Finitude!

["I dwell in Possibility"]

I dwell in Possibility -
A fairer House than Prose -
More numerous of Windows -
Superior - for Doors -

Of Chambers as the Cedars -
Impregnable of Eye -
And for an Everlasting Roof
The Gambrels of the Sky -

Of Visitors - the fairest -
For Occupation - This -
The spreading wide of my narrow Hands
To gather Paradise -

["I've Known a Heaven"]

I've known a Heaven, like a Tent -
To wrap its shining Yards -
Pluck up its stakes, and disappear -
Without the sound of Boards
Or Rip of Nail - Or Carpenter -
But just the miles of Stare -
That signalize a Show's Retreat -
In North America -

No Trace - no Figment of the Thing
That dazzled, Yesterday,
No Ring - no Marvel -
Men, and Feats -
Dissolved as utterly -
As Bird's far Navigation
Discloses just a Hue -
A splash of Oars, a Gaiety -
Then swallowed up, of View.

["Tis wider than the Sky"]

The Brain - is wider than the Sky -
For - put them side by side -
The one the other will contain
With ease - and You - beside -

The Brain is deeper than the sea -
For - hold them - Blue to Blue -
The one the other will absorb -
As Sponges - Buckets - do -

The Brain is just the weight of God -
For - Heft them - Pound for Pound -
And they will differ - if they do -
As Syllable from Sound -

["It might be lonelier"]

It might be lonelier
Without the Loneliness -
I'm so accustomed to my Fate -
Perhaps the Other - Peace -

Would interrupt the Dark -
And crowd the little Room -
Too scant - by Cubits - to contain
The Sacrament - of Him -

I am not used to Hope -
It might intrude upon -
Its sweet parade - blaspheme the place -
Ordained to Suffering -

It might be easier
To fail - with Land in Sight -
Than gain - My Blue Peninsula -
To perish - of Delight -

["Exhilaration – is within"]

Exhilaration – is within –
There can no Outer Wine
So royally intoxicate
As that diviner Brand

The Soul achieves – Herself –
To drink – or set away
For Visitor – Or Sacrament –
'Tis not of Holiday

To stimulate a Man
Who hath the Ample Rhine
Within his Closet – Best you can
Exhale in offering.

["It struck me – every Day"]

It struck me – every Day –
The Lightning was as new
As if the Cloud that instant slit
And let the Fire through –

It burned Me – in the Night –
It Blistered to My Dream –
It sickened fresh upon my sight –
With every Morn that came –

I thought that Storm – was brief –
The Maddest – quickest by –
But Nature lost the Date of This –
And left it in the Sky –

["Lift it – with the Feathers"]

Lift it – with the Feathers
Not alone we fly –
Launch it – the aquatic
Not the only sea –
Advocate the Azure
To the lower Eyes –
He has obligation
Who has Paradise –

["Like Rain it sounded till it curved"]

Like Rain it sounded till it curved
And then I knew 'twas Wind -
It walked as wet as any Wave
But swept as dry as sand -
When it had pushed itself away
To some remotest Plain
A coming as of Hosts was heard
That was indeed the Rain -
It filled the Wells, it pleased the Pools
It warbled in the Road -
It pulled the spigot from the Hills
And let the Floods abroad -
It loosened acres, lifted seas
The sites of Centres stirred
Then like Elijah rode away
Upon a Wheel of Cloud.

["A word is dead"]

A word is dead
When it is said, Some say.

I say it just
Begins to live
That day.

["Go travelling with us!"]

"Go travelling with us!"
Her *travels daily be*
By routes of ecstasy
To Evening's Sea –

["The Thrill came slowly like a Boon"]

The Thrill came slowly like a Boon for
Centuries delayed
Its fitness growing like the Flood
In sumptuous solitude -
The desolation only missed
While Rapture changed its Dress
And stood amazed before the Change
In ravished Holiness -

["And with what body do they come?"]

"And with what body do they come?" -
Then they do *come - Rejoice!*
What Door - What Hour - Run - run - My Soul!
Illuminate the House!

"Body!" Then real - a Face and Eyes -
To know that it is them! -
Paul knew the Man that knew the News -
He passed through Bethlehem -

["Lightly stepped a yellow star"]

Lightly stepped a yellow star
To its lofty place -
Loosed the Moon her silver hat
From her lustral Face -
All of Evening softly lit
As an Astral Hall -
Father, I observed to Heaven,
You are punctual.

["Pass to thy Rendezvous of Light"]

Pass to thy Rendezvous of Light,
Pangless except for us -
Who slowly ford the Mystery
Which thou hast leaped across!

["To wait an Hour - is long"]

To wait an Hour - is long -
If Love be just beyond -
To wait Eternity - is short -
If love reward the end -

["We outgrow love like other things"]

We outgrow love like other things
And put it in the drawer,
Till it an antique fashion shows
Like costumes grandsires wore.

["You left me, sweet, two legacies"]

You left me, sweet, two legacies, -
A legacy of love
A Heavenly Father would content,
Had He the offer of;

You left me boundaries of pain
Capacious as the sea,
Between eternity and time,
Your consciousness and me.

["This is my letter to the world"]

This is my letter to the world,
That never wrote to me, -
The simple news that Nature told,
With tender majesty.

Her message is committed
To hands I cannot see;
For love of her, sweet countrymen,
Judge tenderly of me!

["The pedigree of honey"]

The pedigree of honey
Does not concern the bee;
A clover, any time, to him
Is aristocracy.

["Of all the souls that stand create"]

Of all the souls that stand create
I have elected one.
When sense from spirit files away,
And subterfuge is done;

When that which is and that which was
Apart, intrinsic, stand,
And this brief tragedy of flesh
Is shifted like a sand;

When figures show their royal front
And mists are carved sway, -
Behold the atom I Feferred
To all the lists of clay!

["I like to see it lap the miles"]

I like to see it lap the miles,
And lick the valleys up,
And stop to feed itself at tanks;
And then, prodigious, step

Around a pile of mountains,
And, supercilious, peer
In shanties by the sides of roads;
And then a quarry pare

To fit its sides, and crawl between,
Complaining all the while
In horrid, hooting stanza;
Then chase itself down hill

And neigh like Boanerges;
Then, punctual as a star,
Stop - docile and omnipotent -
At its own stable door.

["To make a prairie"]

To make a prairie it takes a clover and one bee,
One clover, and a bee.
And revery.
The revery alone will do,
If bees are few.

["I taste a liquor never brewed"]

I taste a liquor never brewed -
From Tankards scooped in Pearl -
Not all the Frankfort Berries
Yield such an Alcohol!

Inebriate of air - am I -
And Debauchee of Dew -
Reeling - thro' endless summer days -
From inns of molten Blue -

When "Landlords" turn the drunken Bee
Out of the Foxglove's door -
When Butterflies - renounce their "drams" -
I shall but drink the more!

Till Seraphs swing their snowy Hats -
And Saints - to windows run -
To see the Tippler
Leaning against the - Sun!

["It's all I have to bring today"]

It's all I have to bring today -
This, and my heart beside -
This, and my heart, and all the fields -
And all the meadows wide -
Be sure you count - should I forget
Some one the sum could tell -
This, and my heart, and all the Bees
Which in the Clover dwell.

["The Soul unto itself"]

The Soul unto itself
Is an imperial friend -
Or the most agonizing Spy -
An Enemy - could send -

Secure against its own -
No treason it can fear -
Itself - its Sovereign - of itself
The Soul should stand in Awe -

["It's like the light"]

It's like the light, -
A fashionless delight
It's like the bee, -
A dateless melody.

It's like the woods,
Private like breeze,
Phraseless, yet it stirs
The proudest trees.

It's like the morning, -
Best when it's done, -
The everlasting clocks
Chime noon.

["There is a solitude of space"]

There is a solitude of space
A solitude of sea
A solitude of death, but these
Society shall be
Compared with that profoundest site
That polar privacy
A soul admitted to itself –
Finite infinity.

["Beauty crowds me till I die"]

Beauty crowds me till I die
Beauty mercy have on me
But if I expire today
Let it be in sight of thee –

"Wild Nights! - Wild Nights!"
A Note on Emily Dickinson

Emily Dickinson's poetry is among the strangest, the most compelling and the most direct in world literature. There is nothing else quite like it. She writes in short lyrics, often just eight lines long, often in regular quatrains, but often in irregular lines consisting of two half-lines joined in the middle by a dash (such as: ''Tis Honour - though I die' in "Had I presumed to hope"). Her subjects appear to be the traditional ones of poetry, blocked in with capital letters: God, Love, Hope, Time, Death, Nature, the Sea, the Sun, the World, Childhood, the Past, History, and so on. Yet what exactly is Dickinson discussing? Who is the 'I', the 'Thee', the 'we' and the 'you' in her poetry? This is where things become much more ambiguous. Dickinson is very clear at times in her poetry, until one considers deeper exactly what she is saying - but this ambiguity is one of the hallmarks and the delights of her art.

As an example of Dickinson's idiosyncratic use of punctuation, particularly the dash, this is from "Behind me - dips Eternity":

Behind me - dips Eternity -

> Before Me - Immortality -
> Myself - the Term between -
> Death but the Drift of Eastern Gray,
> Dissolving into Dawn away,
> Before the West begin -

No other poet has made such a distinctive use of the dash, which does for full stops, commas, colons and semi-colons. The dash serves to break up the flow of Dickinson's verse, but it also connects together a series of thoughts. The only other poet I can think of who uses the dash so profusely is Arthur Rimbaud. As with Rimbaud, Dickinson's use of the dash hints at a rush of information, one phrase piling on top of the other. It is a rush of data which's sometimes found in mystical writings. As with Rimbaud, Dickinson's poetry sometimes looks as if she were very excited, as if the experience in the poetry is threatening to break out of the form of the verse. Some poets went for using no punctuation at all (or very little), which we find in modernists such as Ezra Pound or Allen Ginsberg. James Joyce favoured long sentences without internal punctuation, such as quotation marks. Joyce's disciple, Samuel Beckett, wrote whole novels without using much punctuation (*Malone Dies* and *How It Is*), and Beckett's *Unnamable* is written just using the comma to break up blocks of words. The poet's punctuation is part of her/his 'voice' – this is very apparent with Emily Dickinson, and also with poets such as Gertrude Stein, whose dislike of colons, question marks and the like gives her work a distinctive flavour. With Dickinson, though, there is no (or not much) difficulty in understanding how she is trying to speak. There is ambiguity, but it is not the same as the ambiguities in Joyce or Stein. Dickinson also employs a profusion of exclamation marks – as many (if not more) than the equally exuberant Romantic poets. Many more sober poets are wary of exclamation marks, but Dickinson, like the Romantics, was not afraid of using them at all. There is a state that Dickinson's poetic persona gets into, that requires the use of exclamation marks to communicate her exultation. "Wild Nights!

- Wild Nights!" is one of the most ecstatic of Dickinson's poems, and shows how she uses punctuation to achieve the expression of bliss:

Wild Nights! - Wild Nights!
Were I with thee
Wild Nights should be
Our luxury!

Perhaps the oddest part of the form of Dickinson's poetry, though, is her capitalizations. In almost every poem words are capitalized where they do not need to be: 'The World - feels Dusty', 'Drab Habitation of Whom?', 'Sang from the Heart, Sire', 'The Mushroom is the Elf of Plants', 'The pretty Rain from those sweet Eaves'. These lines are the first lines from Dickinson's poems (which also serve as their titles, for her poems are nearly all untitled). It was common practice to capitalize words in poetry up to the 18th century. Robert Herrick, for example, uses capitalizations *and* italics to accentuate words in his famous 'The Argument of His Book':

I sing of *Brooks*, of *Blossomes, Birds*, and *Bowers*:
Of *April, May*, of *June*, and *July-Flowers*...

and it reads as quite normal. In poetry before the 19th century, such capitalizations are part of the poetic tradition. In Dickinson's poetry, though, the capitalized words have a different emphasis.

I have chosen many of Dickinson's more blissful poems - this is a personal preference, of course, but these poems ("Wild Nights - Wild Nights", "Exhilaration - is within", "Title divine - is mine!", "'Tis so much joy! 'Tis so much joy!", "Me - come! My dazzled face") are peculiar to Dickinson, and need to be included in any selection of her verse. The short, compressed lyrics of exaltation are some of the most intense expressions of spiritual feeling in the language. Dickinson is very much a religious poet, but in her own special way. She does not deal with religious sensibility in the hushed reverential and occasionally ecstatic fashion of the British Metaphysical poets (Donne, Herbert, Vaughan, Traherne), nor is she quite like her contemporaries (Whitman, Emerson, Clare, Tennyson and Longfellow). One thinks of Elizabeth Barrett Browning and Christina Rossetti, but even here Dickinson is quite on her own. David Daiches comments:

> Emily Dickinson's poetry is religious in a highly idiosyncratic way. It is neither devotional nor doctrinal. It does not brood, like so much in Tennyson and Arnold, nor does it work by accumulation and expansiveness like the poetry of her contemporary and fellow-American Walt Whitman. Her aim is not to mirror the totally responsive self, as Whitman's is, nor is it the musing self of the Victorians or the disciplined counterpointing of sensuous and religious response we find in Gerald Manley Hopkins: it is the innocent utterance of one for whom categories of existence are tested wholly and solely by personal experience.[1]

Dickinson's poetry is tremendously religiously exalted at times, but the details are not clear. What is the source of this ecstasy? God? Love? Life? Nature? One is not certain, either, about the identity of the personages in Dickinson's poetry. The 'He' or 'Him' who frequently appears is usually identified with God, but may refer to a more diffuse sense of deity, something akin to a pantheistic view of Nature. Then there is the question of eroticism and love in Dickinson's poetry. Certainly it is a sexy poetry, the expressions of feeling are often very sensual. Love poetry is founded on absence. The love poem becomes the stand-in for the presence of the beloved. Or as Emily Dickinson put it: 'So we must meet apart'. Love poetry luxuriates in the ambiguities and conflicts of love: it arises out of the very paradoxes that make love such a piquant topic for the artist. Emily Dickinson wrote of this erotic paradox in her poem "I cannot live with You", which, with its strange capitalizations and punctuation, and the Dickinson dash breaking up (or aiding) the flow of emotion, is ambiguous about the ambiguity of love, whether secular or sacred, erotic or Christian:

> So we must meet apart
> You there - I here -
> With just the Door ajar
> That Oceans are - and Prayer -

Dickinson's poem included here, "Wild Nights! - Wild Nights!", seems to be a more straight forward evocation of lust and erotic luxury. But, as Jan Montefiore comments, the poem

> evokes a discharge of energy sensed as forbidden excess, but it is entirely ambiguous whether the luxury is the storm of desire or the promise of shelter from it.[2]

Love poems mark an intersection between language and experience, between desire and gratification, between reality and dream. Many love poems are formed within a space of tension, a tension created by the poet and her/his desire. In Emily Dickinson's art we receive a strong impression of the presence of the poet.[3] One can practically see her composing her lines as she looks out of the window at the sky, the trees and the world.[4] One sees her recollecting history and dreaming of voyages on distant seas. One finds her contemplating the deity, wondering about bringing Him jewels. One sees her musing upon death, time, mortality and eternity. Always, though, the poet's 'I' is shifting. The yearning in Dickinson's poesie, which's sometimes wildly excessive and difficult to sustain, is for any number of targets: for Nature, for God, for love, for the beloved, for distant climes. Dickinson's Christianity, too, is not straightforward, but decidedly ambiguous. The many references to the Bible attest to her deep knowledge of it, but Dickinson's sense of irony and ambiguity ensure that the Old Testament allusions are seldom rendered in an orthodox manner.

Notes

1. David Daiches: *God and the Poets: The Gifford Lectures, 1983,* Clarendon Press, Oxford, 1984, 160
2. *Feminism and Poetry: Language, Experience, Identity in Women's Writing,* Jan Montefiore, Pandora, 1994, 168
3. Dickinson's poetic persona delights in solitude. How much the persona fits the reality of Dickinson's life is a point much debated. Adrienne Rich writes: 'I have a notion that genius knows itself; that Dickinson chose her seclusion, knowing that she was exceptional and knowing what she needed. It was, moreover, no hermetic retreat, but a seclusion which included a wide range of people, of reading and correspondence.' (Rich: "Vesuvius at Home: The Power of Emily Dickinson", in S. Gilbert & S. Gubar, eds: *Shakespeare's Sisters: Feminist Essays on Women Poets,* Indiana University Press 1979, 100)
4. Dickinson's room at Amherst, Massachusetts, was the best bedroom in the house, according to Adrienne Rich; it was a sunny, corner room, with potted plants and a work table. (ib.)

J.R.R. Tolkien
The Books, The Films, The Whole Cultural Phenomenon

by Jeremy Mark Robinson

A new critical study of J.R.R. Tolkien, creator of Middle-earth and author of *The Lord of the Rings, The Hobbit* and *The Silmarillion*, among other books.

This new critical study explores Tolkien's major writings (*The Lord of the Rings, The Hobbit, Beowulf: The Monster and the Critics, The Letters, The Silmarillion* and *The History of Middle-earth* volumes); Tolkien and fairy tales; the mythological, political and religious aspects of Tolkien's Middle-earth; the critics' response to Tolkien's fiction over the decades; the Tolkien industry (merchandizing, toys, role-playing games, posters, Tolkien societies, conferences and the like); Tolkien in visual and fantasy art; the cultural aspects of The Lord of the Rings (from the 1950s to the present); Tolkien's fiction's relationship with other fantasy fiction, such as C.S. Lewis and *Harry Potter*; and the TV, radio and film versions of Tolkien's books, including the 2001-03 Hollywood interpretations of *The Lord of the Rings*.

This new book draws on contemporary cultural theory and analysis and offers a sympathetic and illuminating (and sceptical) account of the Tolkien phenomenon. This book is designed to appeal to the general reader (and viewer) of Tolkien: it is written in a clear, jargon-free and easily-accessible style.

754pp   ISBN 1-86171-057-7   £25.00 / $37.50

The Best of Peter Redgrove's Poetry
The Book of Wonders

by Peter Redgrove, edited and introduced by Jeremy Robinson

Poems of wet shirts and 'wonder-awakening dresses'; honey, wasps and bees; orchards and apples; rivers, seas and tides; storms, rain, weather and clouds; waterworks; labyrinths; amazing perfumes; the Cornish landscape (Penzance, Perranporth, Falmouth, Boscastle, the Lizard and Scilly Isles); the sixth sense and 'extra-sensuous perception'; witchcraft; alchemical vessels and laboratories; yoga; menstruation; mines, minerals and stones; sand dunes; mud-baths; mythology; dreaming; vulvas; and lots of sex magic. This book gathers together poetry (and prose) from every stage of Redgrove's career, and every book. It includes pieces that have only appeared in small presses and magazines, and in uncollected form.

'Peter Redgrove is really an extraordinary poet' (George Szirtes, Quarto magazine)
'Peter Redgrove is one of the few significant poets now writing... His 'means' are indeed brilliant and delightful. Technically he is a poet essentially of brilliant and unexpected images...he never disappoints' (Kathleen Raine, Temenos magazine).

240pp   ISBN 1-86171-063-1   2nd edition   £19.99 / $29.50

Sex–Magic–Poetry–Cornwall
A Flood of Poems

by Peter Redgrove. Edited with an essay by Jeremy Robinson

A marvellous collection of poems by one of Britain's best but underrated poets, Peter Redgrove. This book brings together some of Redgrove's wildest and most passionate works, creating a 'flood' of poetry. Philip Hobsbaum called Redgrove 'the great poet of our time', while Angela Carter said: 'Redgrove's language can light up a page.' Redgrove ranks alongside Ted Hughes and Sylvia Plath. He is in every way a 'major poet'. Robinson's essay analyzes all of Redgrove's poetic work, including his use of sex magic, natural science, menstruation, psychology, myth, alchemy and feminism.
A new edition, including a new introduction, new preface and new bibliography.

'Robinson's enthusiasm is winning, and his perceptive readings are supported by a very useful bibliography' (Acumen magazine)
'Sex-Magic-Poetry-Cornwall is a very rich essay... It is like a brightly-lighted box. (Peter Redgrove)
'This is an excellent selection of poetry and an extensive essay on the themes and theories of this unusual poet by Jeremy Robinson' (Chapman magazine)

220pp   New, 3rd edition   ISBN 1-86171-070-4   £14.99 / $23.50

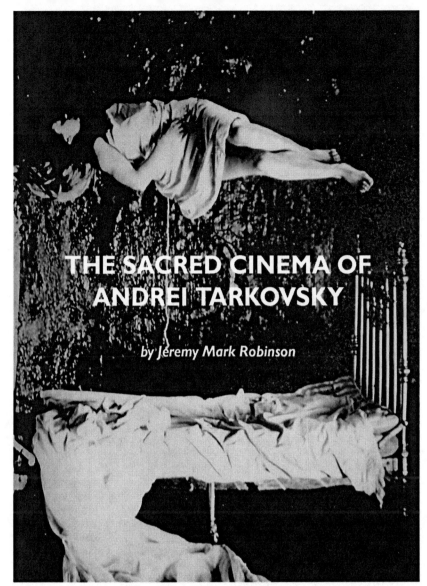

THE SACRED CINEMA OF ANDREI TARKOVSKY

by Jeremy Mark Robinson

A new study of the Russian filmmaker Andrei Tarkovsky (1932-1986), director of seven feature films, including *Andrei Roublyov, Mirror, Solaris, Stalker* and *The Sacrifice*.
This is one of the most comprehensive and detailed studies of Tarkovsky's cinema available. Every film is explored in depth, with scene-by-scene analyses. All aspects of Tarkovsky's output are critiqued, including editing, camera, staging, script, budget, collaborations, production, sound, music, performance and spirituality. Tarkovsky is placed with a European New Wave tradition of filmmaking, alongside directors like Ingmar Bergman, Carl Theodor Dreyer, Pier Paolo Pasolini and Robert Bresson.
An essential addition to film studies.

Illustrations: 150 b/w, 4 colour. 682 pages. First edition. Hardback.

Publisher: Crescent Moon Publishing. Distributor: Gardners Books.

ISBN 1-86171-096-8 (9781861710963) £60.00 / $105.00

THE ART OF ANDY GOLDSWORTHY

COMPLETE WORKS: SPECIAL EDITION
(PAPERBACK and HARDBACK)

by William Malpas

A new, special edition of the study of the contemporary British sculptor, Andy Goldsworthy, including a new introduction, new bibliography and many new illustrations.

This is the most comprehensive, up-to-date, well-researched and in-depth account of Goldsworthy's art available anywhere.

Andy Goldsworthy makes land art. His sculpture is a sensitive, intuitive response to nature, light, time, growth, the seasons and the earth. Goldsworthy's environmental art is becoming ever more popular: 1993's art book *Stone* was a bestseller; the press raved about Goldsworthy taking over a number of London West End art galleries in 1994; during 1995 Goldsworthy designed a set of Royal Mail stamps and had a show at the British Museum. Malpas surveys all of Goldsworthy's art, and analyzes his relation with other land artists such as Robert Smithson, Walter de Maria, Richard Long and David Nash, and his place in the contemporary British art scene.

The Art of Andy Goldsworthy discusses all of Goldsworthy's important and recent exhibitions and books, including the *Sheepfolds* project; the TV documentaries; *Wood* (1996); the New York Holocaust memorial (2003); and Goldsworthy's collaboration on a dance performance.

Illustrations: 70 b/w, 1 colour: 330 pages. New, special, 2nd edition.
Publisher: Crescent Moon Publishing. Distributor: Gardners Books.

ISBN 1-86171-059-3 (9781861710598) (Paperback) £25.00 / $44.00

ISBN 1-86171-080-1 (9781861710802) (Hardback) £60.00 / $105.00

CRESCENT MOON PUBLISHING

ARTS, PAINTING, SCULPTURE

The Art of Andy Goldsworthy: Complete Works(Pbk)
The Art of Andy Goldsworthy: Complete Works (Hbk)
Andy Goldsworthy in Close-Up (Pbk)
Andy Goldsworthy in Close-Up (Hbk)
Land Art: A Complete Guide
Richard Long: The Art of Walking
The Art of Richard Long: Complete Works (Pbk)
The Art of Richard Long: Complete Works (Hbk)
Richard Long in Close-Up
Land Art In the UK
Land Art in Close-Up
Installation Art in Close-Up
Minimal Art and Artists In the 1960s and After
Colourfield Painting
Land Art DVD, TV documentary
Andy Goldsworthy DVD, TV documentary
The Erotic Object: Sexuality in Sculpture From Prehistory to the Present Day
Sex in Art: Pornography and Pleasure in Painting and Sculpture
Postwar Art
Sacred Gardens: The Garden in Myth, Religion and Art
Glorification: Religious Abstraction in Renaissance and 20th Century Art
Early Netherlandish Painting
Leonardo da Vinci
Piero della Francesca
Giovanni Bellini
Fra Angelico: Art and Religion in the Renaissance
Mark Rothko: The Art of Transcendence
Frank Stella: American Abstract Artist
Jasper Johns: Painting By Numbers
Brice Marden
Alison Wilding: The Embrace of Sculpture
Vincent van Gogh: Visionary Landscapes
Eric Gill: Nuptials of God
Constantin Brancusi: Sculpting the Essence of Things
Max Beckmann
Egon Schiele: Sex and Death In Purple Stockings
Delizioso Fotografico Fervore: Works In Process 1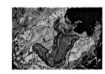
Sacro Cuore: Works In Process 2
The Light Eternal: J.M.W. Turner
The Madonna Glorified: Karen Arthurs

LITERATURE

J.R.R. Tolkien: The Books, The Films, The Whole Cultural Phenomenon
Harry Potter
Sexing Hardy: Thomas Hardy and Feminism
Thomas Hardy's *Tess of the d'Urbervilles*
Thomas Hardy's *Jude the Obscure*
Thomas Hardy: The Tragic Novels
Love and Tragedy: Thomas Hardy
The Poetry of Landscape in Hardy
Wessex Revisited: Thomas Hardy and John Cowper Powys
Wolfgang Iser: Essays
Petrarch, Dante and the Troubadours
Maurice Sendak and the Art of Children's Book Illustration
Andrea Dworkin
Cixous, Irigaray, Kristeva: The *Jouissance* of French Feminism
Julia Kristeva: Art, Love, Melancholy, Philosophy, Semiotics and Psychoanalysis
Hélene Cixous I Love You: The *Jouissance* of Writing
Luce Irigaray: Lips, Kissing, and the Politics of Sexual Difference
Peter Redgrove: Here Comes the Flood
Peter Redgrove: Sex-Magic-Poetry-Cornwall
Lawrence Durrell: Between Love and Death, East and West
Love, Culture & Poetry: Lawrence Durrell
Cavafy: Anatomy of a Soul
German Romantic Poetry: Goethe, Novalis, Heine, Hölderlin, Schlegel, Schiller
Feminism and Shakespeare
Shakespeare: Selected Sonnets
Shakespeare: Love, Poetry & Magic
The Passion of D.H. Lawrence
D.H. Lawrence: Symbolic Landscapes
D.H. Lawrence: Infinite Sensual Violence
Rimbaud: Arthur Rimbaud and the Magic of Poetry
The Ecstasies of John Cowper Powys
Sensualism and Mythology: The Wessex Novels of John Cowper Powys
Amorous Life: John Cowper Powys and the Manifestation of Affectivity (H.W. Fawkner)
Postmodern Powys: New Essays on John Cowper Powys (Joe Boulter)
Rethinking Powys: Critical Essays on John Cowper Powys
Paul Bowles & Bernardo Bertolucci
Rainer Maria Rilke
In the Dim Void: Samuel Beckett
Samuel Beckett Goes into the Silence
André Gide: Fiction and Fervour
Jackie Collins and the Blockbuster Novel
Blinded By Her Light: The Love-Poetry of Robert Graves
The Passion of Colours: Travels In Mediterranean Lands
Poetic Forms
The Dolphin-Boy

POETRY

The Best of Peter Redgrove's Poetry
Peter Redgrove: Here Comes The Flood
Peter Redgrove: Sex-Magic-Poetry-Cornwall
Ursula Le Guin: Walking In Cornwall
Dante: Selections From the Vita Nuova
Petrarch, Dante and the Troubadours
William Shakespeare: Selected Sonnets
Blinded By Her Light: The Love-Poetry of Robert Graves
Emily Dickinson: Selected Poems
Emily Brontë: Poems
Thomas Hardy: Selected Poems
Percy Bysshe Shelley: Poems
John Keats: Selected Poems
D.H. Lawrence: Selected Poems
Edmund Spenser: Poems
John Donne: Poems
Henry Vaughan: Poems
Sir Thomas Wyatt: Poems
Robert Herrick: Selected Poems
Rilke: Space, Essence and Angels in the Poetry of Rainer Maria Rilke
Rainer Maria Rilke: Selected Poems
Friedrich Hölderlin: Selected Poems
Arseny Tarkovsky: Selected Poems
Arthur Rimbaud: Selected Poems
Arthur Rimbaud: A Season in Hell
Arthur Rimbaud and the Magic of Poetry
D.J. Enright: By-Blows
Jeremy Reed: Brigitte's Blue Heart
Jeremy Reed: Claudia Schiffer's Red Shoes
Gorgeous Little Orpheus
Radiance: New Poems
Crescent Moon Book of Nature Poetry
Crescent Moon Book of Love Poetry
Crescent Moon Book of Mystical Poetry
Crescent Moon Book of Elizabethan Love Poetry
Crescent Moon Book of Metaphysical Poetry
Crescent Moon Book of Romantic Poetry
Pagan America: New American Poetry

MEDIA, CINEMA, FEMINISM and CULTURAL STUDIES

J.R.R. Tolkien: The Books, The Films, The Whole Cultural Phenomenon
Harry Potter
Cixous, Irigaray, Kristeva: The *Jouissance* of French Feminism
Julia Kristeva: Art, Love, Melancholy, Philosophy, Semiotics and Psychoanalysis
Luce Irigaray: Lips, Kissing, and the Politics of Sexual Difference
Hélene Cixous I Love You: The *Jouissance* of Writing
Andrea Dworkin
'Cosmo Woman': The World of Women's Magazines
Women in Pop Music
Discovering the Goddess (Geoffrey Ashe)
The Poetry of Cinema
The Sacred Cinema of Andrei Tarkovsky (Pbk and Hbk)
Paul Bowles & Bernardo Bertolucci
Media Hell: Radio, TV and the Press
An Open Letter to the BBC
Detonation Britain: Nuclear War in the UK
Feminism and Shakespeare
Wild Zones: Pornography, Art and Feminism
Sex in Art: Pornography and Pleasure in Painting and Sculpture
Sexing Hardy: Thomas Hardy and Feminism

In my view *The Light Eternal* is among the very best of all the material I read on Turner. (Douglas Graham, director of the Turner Museum, Denver, Colorado)

The Light Eternal is a model monograph, an exemplary job. The subject matter of the book is beautifully organised and dead on beam. (Lawrence Durrell)

It is amazing for me to see my work treated with such passion and respect. (Andrea Dworkin)

Sex-Magic-Poetry-Cornwall is a very rich essay... It is like a brightly-lighted box. (Peter Redgrove)

CRESCENT MOON PUBLISHING
P.O. Box 393, Maidstone, Kent, ME14 5XU, United Kingdom.
01622-729593 (UK) 01144-1622-729593 (US) 0044-1622-729593 (other territories)
cresmopub@yahoo.co.uk   www.crescentmoon.org.uk

Printed in the United Kingdom
by Lightning Source UK Ltd.
130216UK00001B/1/P